THE

SNOW-STORM;

OR,

An Account

OF

THE NATURE, PROPERTIES, DANGERS,
AND USES OF SNOW,

IN VARIOUS PARTS OF THE WORLD.

———

PUBLISHED UNDER THE DIRECTION OF
THE COMMITTEE OF GENERAL LITERATURE AND EDUCATION
APPOINTED BY THE SOCIETY FOR PROMOTING
CHRISTIAN KNOWLEDGE.

———

LONDON:
Printed for the
SOCIETY FOR PROMOTING CHRISTIAN KNOWLEDGE;
SOLD AT THE DEPOSITORY,
GREAT QUEEN STREET, LINCOLN'S INN FIELDS,
AND 4, ROYAL EXCHANGE.
1845.

SNOW

Pleasant to the sober'd soul
The silence of the wintry scene,
When nature shrouds herself, entranc'd
In deep tranquillity.—SOUTHEY.

CONTENTS.

CHAPTER I.
P. 9.

CHAPTER II.
P. 49.

CONTENTS.

SERVANT AND DOGS OF ST. BERNARD ON DUTY.

THE SNOW-STORM.

CHAPTER I.

"I saw the woods and fields at close of day
A variegated show; the meadows green,
Though faded; and the lands, where lately waved
The golden harvest, of a mellow brown,
Upturn'd so lately by the forceful share.
I saw far off the weedy fallows smile
With verdure not unprofitable, grazed
By flocks, fast feeding, and selecting each
His favourite herb; while all the leafless groves

That skirt the horizon, wore a sable hue,
Scarce noticed in the kindred dusk of eve.
To-morrow brings a change ! a total change!
Which even now, though silently perform'd,
And slowly, and by most unfelt, the face
Of universal nature undergoes.
Fast falls a fleecy shower : the downy flakes.
Descending, and, with never ceasing lapse,
Softly alighting upon all below,
Assimilate all objects. Earth receives
Gladly the thickening mantle ; and the green
And tender blade, that fear'd the chilling blast,
Escapes unhurt beneath so warm a veil."—COWPER.

To the inhabitants of hot countries, it is quite impossible to form any correct ideas of the nature and appearance of a snow-storm, and when such persons are permitted in more temperate climates to behold this remarkable spectacle, they generally exhibit the greatest astonishment and admiration. Nor would our own sensations be very different from theirs, had we not been from childhood so accustomed to witness falls of snow, and perhaps to regret their interference with our usual pastimes, as to lose the feelings which might naturally be excited thereby. The rapid descent of snow-flakes through the sky, is a sight that, to the well-housed and well-clad, is certainly one of beauty.

" Thick fall the floating flakes, as light,
As fine, as soft, as pure, as white,

> As the wind-waver'd egret's crest;
> Or the warm down that lines the breast
> Of swans, or hyperborean geese,
> By winter bleach'd; or like the fleece,
> Fresh from the stream, that whitens o'er,
> Heaps upon heaps, the shearing floor;
> What time the jocund shepherd's cull
> From summer flocks, their weight of wool."—MANT.

Gradually and silently a change comes over the face of nature. First, a thin and slight covering veils all objects, leaving their forms still visible; but soon this covering becomes more dense, and all forms lose their distinctness. The trim borders, the verdant lawn, the level pathway, the furrowed field, the yet remaining tufts of herbage, and even the way-side banks and humbler fences begin to melt into a smooth and equal surface of brilliant whiteness.

> "About each humble shrub below,
> Step after step the gathering snow
> From leaf to leaf, from bough to bough,
> Creeps up with silent pace; and now
> It meets the topmost spike above,
> And wraps them in an ambient cove.
> The dykes that bordering lands divide,
> The bank that skirts the sloping side,
> Along the field the hedgerow bush,
> Fringing the pool the waving rush,
> Feel by degrees the snow pile spread,
> Ascend their sides, surmount their head."—MANT.

And now, too, all sounds are muffled : the village
bells seem to be at a greater distance, so faintly
do their tones fall upon the ear; the waggon that
yesterday grated so harshly against the stones,
now moves along in silence; the footsteps of pas-
sengers are not heard; and though you see people
walking or riding about as usual, yet, hearing no
noise, you are reminded of the moving scenes of a
panorama rather than the real proceedings of life.

Under this apparently cold mantle, most small
plants lie secure; they are protected by it from
the severity of the frost, and in this shelter they
nourish and prepare their young shoots to re-
appear above ground in the spring. Meanwhile
the deep snow while newly-fallen gives matchless
purity and brightness to the wintry landscape.

> " The cherished fields
> Put on their winter robe of purest white.
> 'Tis brightness all : save where the new snow melts
> Along the mazy current. Low the woods
> Bow their hoar head ; and ere the languid sun,
> Faint from the west, emits his evening ray,
> Earth's universal face, deep hid and chill,
> Is one wide dazzling waste that buries deep
> The works of man."

Beautiful as this may be to the eye, it is accompanied with a sense of dreariness to those who

have to journey through the country thus overwhelmed; and if the traveller be overtaken by
darkness, and by a renewal of the storm, his position becomes not only painful but dangerous.   It
is in mountainous countries that the greatest
danger is to be apprehended; but even in England there have been instances of fatal accidents
thus occurring.   The case of Elizabeth Wood-
cock, who was buried in snow for eight days near
Cambridge, attracted much notice at the time of
its occurrence in 1799.   This poor woman was
returning on horseback from Cambridge to her
own home, and was only half a mile distant from
the desired spot, when her horse became frightened
at a sudden light, perhaps of a meteor, and she
dismounted with the intention of leading him
home.

It was seven o'clock in the evening of the 2d
of February, and there had been much snow all
day, so that the roads and lanes were deeply
covered, and ditches were filled up.   The woman
was fatigued and unable to manage the wayward
horse, which broke loose and went home.   Half
benumbed with cold, she felt that she could proceed no farther without resting.   She therefore

sat down under a thicket where there was not much snow. But it rapidly accumulated, and in an hour's time had completely hemmed her in. Her clothes became stiffened by the frost, and she was wholly unable to escape from her perilous situation. Night came on, and a kind of drowsiness prevented her from feeling the horror of her position. In the morning she was buried in snow to the depth of six feet, having two or three feet of snow above her head. A small opening in this snowy roof admitted day-light, and the woman managed to push through it a twig from the bush against which she leaned, having first fastened her handkerchief to the top. After this effort she seems to have relapsed into a state of torpor and despondency, in which she remained all the succeeding days and nights; for, although she was quite aware of the ringing of the church bells, and the usual sounds of her village, and could even distinguish the voices of persons passing near the spot, and hear the subject of their conversation, she was nevertheless unable to make any effectual effort to gain their attention, and they unfortunately did not observe the handkerchief she had hoisted as a signal of distress.

She once tried to take a pinch of snuff, but she found great pain and difficulty in raising her hand to her head, and was also unable to find the usual gratification in the snuff. She also contrived to take off her two wedding-rings, and placed them, with her money, in a small box which she happened to have with her, thinking they would thus be safer, in case of her dying before she was discovered. On the fifth day of her imprisonment a thaw commenced, but this only added to her miseries, for although the hole in the roof was considerably enlarged thereby, yet the dripping of the melted snow on her garments, and their increased weight, made her faint and languid. On making an effort to move, she found that her feet and legs were no longer obedient to her will, and she sank back again in despair. Her sufferings now greatly increased; hope forsook her; and she remained until the period of her discovery, in a state which seemed to betoken approaching death. On Sunday, the 10th of February, a young man returning from Cambridge at mid-day, happened to observe the handkerchief hanging upon a twig, and approaching the spot, he heard a sound as of difficult breathing, and soon perceived the poor

woman who had been so long missing. Procuring
assistance, he quickly removed the snow, and
caused her to be wrapped in blankets, and removed
to her own home. Restoratives were cautiously
administered, and the woman partially recovered,
but her feet were found to be in a sadly mutilated
condition, and she lost all the toes, together with
the integuments from the bottom of one foot. She
lingered five months from the period of her discovery, and died July 13th, 1799.

The snow-storms of Scotland are much more
violent than any experienced in this portion of
the kingdom, and accidents such as the above are
consequently less rare. There is something truly
awful in a storm of snow among the hills in spring.
The following is a description of one by an accu-
rate observer:—" In the evening, after a day of
unwonted tranquillity, dense clouds appear like
great snowy mountains in the western part of the
horizon, while the few clouds which lie in streaks
across the setting sun are intensely deep in their
shadows, and equally bright in their lights. As
the evening closes in, the clouds disappear; the
stars are unusually brilliant, and there is not a
breath of air stirring. The old experienced farmer

goes out to take his wonted nocturnal survey of the heavens, from which long observation on the same spot has enabled him to form a tolerably correct judgment of what will be the state of the weather in the morning. Two or three meteors—brilliant, but of short duration—shoot along a quadrant of the sky, as if they were so many bright lights of the firmament dropping from their orbits. He returns, and directs his men to prepare for what may happen, as there will certainly be a change in the weather. The air is perfectly tranquil when the family retire to their early pillows, to find that repose which healthful labour sweetens, and never misses,—

'Till rest, delicious, chase each transient pain,
And new-born vigour swell in every vein.

But just at the turn of the night the south gives way, the north triumphs, and the whirlwind, herald of victory, lays hold of the four corners of the house, and shakes it with the shaking of an earthquake. But the house, like its inhabitants, is made for the storm, and to stand secure and harmless, while the wind thunders in the fields around, every gust roaring louder than another amongst the leafless branches of the stately trees.

B

In a little its sound is muffled, without being
lessened, and the snow is heard battering at the
windows for an entrance, but battering in vain.
Morning dawns; but every lea and eddy is
wreathed up; the snow still darkens the air, and
reeks along the curling wreaths as if each were a
furnace. For two days and two nights the storm
rages with unabated violence; but on the third
day the wind has veered more easterly, blows
rather feebly, and though the snow falls as thickly,
it falls uniformly over the whole surface. This
continues for two or three days more; and on the
coming of the last of these days, the sun, which
has not been visible for nearly a week, looks out
just before setting, as if promising a morning visit.
The night remains clear, with keen frost; and the
wind steady at north, and blowing very gently.
The sun rises bright in the morning; the storm is
over; and the weather remains unbroken for four
or five weeks."

The state of mind induced among the peasantry
by these storms is thus pleasingly described by the
Ettrick Shepherd. "The daily feelings naturally
impressed upon the shepherd's mind, that all his com-
forts are so entirely in the hands of Him who rules

the elements, contributes not a little to that firm
spirit of devotion for which the Scottish Shepherd is
so distinguished.   I know of no scene so impressive
as that of a family sequestered in a lone glen
during the time of a winter storm; and where is
the glen in the kingdom that wants such a habitation? There they are left to the protection of
heaven; and they know and feel it.   Throughout
all the wild vicissitudes of nature, they have no
hope of assistance from man, but expect to receive
it from the Almighty alone.   Before retiring to
rest, the Shepherd uniformly goes out to examine
the state of the weather, and make his report to
the little dependent group within; nothing is to
be seen but the conflict of the elements, nor heard
but the raving of the storm.   Then they all kneel
around him while he commends them to the protection of heaven; and though their little hymn
of praise can scarcely be heard even by themselves,
as it mixes with the roar of the tempest, they
never fail to rise from their devotions with their
spirits cheered, and their confidence restored, and
go to sleep with an exaltation of mind of which
kings and conquerors have no share."

Of these storms, that of 1794 may be noticed

as one of the most extraordinary with which Scotland was ever visited.   It occurred in the night of
the 24th of January.   The early part of the night
there was a dead calm, with a very slight fall of
snow ; but at two o'clock in the morning, a sudden
and most violent storm commenced ; the air was
completely overloaded with falling and driving
snow, and in a very short space of time, glens
and hollows were filled up, flocks buried, and
dwelling houses walled up to their roofs.   The
next day the darkness was so great that it was
impossible to see twenty yards around, and the
search after the buried flocks was a most perilous
adventure, seeing that in many of the glens the
snow was so deep as to conceal every vestige of
the lofty forest trees which grew there.   By this
one night's snow storm, seventeen shepherds in the
south of Scotland lost their lives, while thirty or
forty were saved with difficulty, after they had
become insensible.   One farmer lost seventy-two
scores of sheep, and many others from twenty to
thirty scores each.   In some cases, whole flocks
were overwhelmed, and were not discovered until
the melting snow exposed their dead bodies.
Hundreds of sheep were driven by the violence of

the storm into waters, burns and lakes, where they were buried or frozen up, and then carried away by the succeeding floods. In a kind of shoal, called the beds of Esk, where several streams flow into the Solway Frith, there were found after the storm, the dead bodies of two men, one woman, forty-five dogs, three horses, nine black cattle, one hundred and eighty hares, and eighteen hundred and forty sheep.

The search after lost sheep when a snow-storm has subsided, is carried on in one of the two following ways. Three or four persons carrying shovels and long smooth poles, walk in company along the surface of the drifted snow, under which they suspect the animals to lie buried, frequently pushing their poles gently through the snow, and thus feeling after the missing sheep. This is called *prodding* or probing for sheep, and persons accustomed to it can readily distinguish, by the touch of the pole, the woolly coat of the sheep, from heath or moss, or any other substance which might seem to resemble it; as soon as the discovery is made, the whole party set to work with shovels to clear the snow. This mode of search is, however, extremely slow and tedious, a great

deal of time being wasted in examining a small
space, while the drifts are often of great extent.
The better course is, therefore, to employ dogs in
searching for the sheep; and some of the shepherds' dogs of Scotland show extraordinary sagacity
in this particular. When a dog becomes noted
for his skill as a sheep-finder, he is in general
request after a snow-storm, and is frequently bor-
rowed or hired for the necessary service. The
conduct of one of these animals is thus described
by his owner:—"The sagacious animal always
took advantage of the wind, where that was prac-
ticable, and the moment he was told to 'seek the
sheep—be careful,' his whole attention was bestowed upon those parts of the snowdrift that the
parties pointed out to him. With his nose close
to the surface of the snow, his eyes beaming with
intelligence, and anxiously watching every motion
of the person that accompanied him, his ears in an
attitude of listening, as if he expected to assist
the sense of smelling by that of hearing, would he
traverse the hard, soft, or slippery snow-drift.
When he first ascertained that there were buried
sheep somewhere in the vicinity, he would then
examine, with peculiar caution, every part of the

surrounding surface, until he appeared to have satisfied himself regarding the precise locality, and then he would commence scratching away the snow with all his might. This was a sure signal for those who carried the shovels to commence digging, but the dog was never satisfied unless he were allowed to continue his scratching, as if he were anxious to set the imprisoned sheep at liberty as soon as possible."

The snow storms of this northern portion of our kingdom were doubtless in the mind of the poet Thomson, when he wrote the following true and touching lines :—

" Now, shepherds, to your helpless charge be kind,
  Baffle the raging year, and fill their pens
  With food at will; lodge them below the storm,
  And watch them strict : for from the bellowing east,
  In this dire season, oft the whirlwind's wing
  Sweeps up the burden of whole wintry plains
  At one wide waft, and o'er the hapless flocks,
  Hid in the hollow of two neighbouring hills,
  The billowy tempest whelms; till, upward urged,
  The valley to a shining mountain swells,
  Tipp'd with a wreath, high-curling in the sky.
      As thus the snows arise ; and foul and fierce,
  All winter drives along the darken'd air;
  In his own loose revolving fields, the swain
  Disaster'd stands ; sees other hills ascend,

Of unknown joyless brow ; and other scenes,
Of horrid prospect, shag the trackless plain :
Nor finds the river, nor the forest, hid
Beneath the formless wild ; but wanders on
From hill to dale, still more and more astray ;
Impatient flouncing through the drifted heaps,
Stung with the thoughts of home ; the thoughts of home
Rush on his nerves, and call their vigour forth
In many a vain attempt.   How sinks his soul !
What black despair, what horror fills his heart !
When for the dusky spot, which fancy feign'd
His tufted cottage rising through the snow,
He meets the roughness of the middle waste,
Far from the track and bless'd abode of man ;
While round him, night resistless closes fast,
And every tempest howling o'er his head
Renders the savage wilderness more wild."

But even the snow-storms of Scotland appear
less formidable when compared with those of the
Andes.   In the passage over these mountains the
traveller finds a number of brick huts, built as
places of shelter during the tempest.   But these
are sometimes insufficient to save from destruction those who take refuge in them.   " The
storms," says Captain Head, " are so violent that
no animal can live in them : there is no warning,
but all of a sudden the snow is seen coming over
the tops of the mountains in a hurricane of wind.

Hundreds of people have been lost in these storms; several had been starved in the hut where we stopped to rest, and only two years before, the winter, by suddenly setting in, had shut up the passage across the mountain, and had driven ten poor travellers to this hut. When the violence of the first storms had subsided, the courier came to the spot, and found six of the ten lying dead in the hut, and by their sides the other four, almost dead with hunger and cold. They had eaten their mules and their dog; and the bones of these animals were now before us."

The same writer gives a vivid picture of a snow-storm in Canada, which he encountered when on a journey in the depth of winter. The track over which he travelled had not yet been settled; no roads were, therefore, to be had, and the ground was either too rough, or the snow too deep, for a sledge or a sleigh, except one adapted for baggage only, called a *tobogin*. The party, therefore, chose the frozen surface of a river as the smoothest track. They moved heavily along upon their snow-shoes, hardly speaking, except when, at the end of each half-hour, it became necessary to exchange places with the leading man, whose

office, in opening a path for the others, was very
laborious. A snow-storm had been gathering
during the day : " Still, however, we went on, and
it grew darker and darker, till a heavy fall of
snow, driven by a powerful wind, came sweeping
along the desert track, directly in our teeth; so
that, what with general fatigue, and the unaccus-
tomed position of the body in the snow-shoes,
I hardly could bear up, and stand against it. The
dreary howling of the tempest, over the wide waste
of snow, rendered the scene even still more deso-
late ; and, with the unmitigated prospect before
us of cold and hunger, our party plodded on in
sullen silence, each, in his own mind, well aware
that it was utterly impracticable to reach that
night the place of our destination.

" But, in spite of every obstacle, the strength
of the two Canadians was astonishing; with bodies
bent forward, and leaning on their collar, on they
marched, drawing the tobogins after them with a
firm, indefatigable step; and we had all walked
a little more than seven hours, when the snow-
storm had increased to such a pitch of violence
that it seemed impossible for any human creature
to withstand it; it bid defiance even to their most

extraordinary exertions. The wind now blew a hurricane. We were unable to see each other at a greater distance than ten yards, and the drift gave an appearance to the surface of the snow we were passing over like that of an agitated sea. Wheeled round every now and then by the wind, we were enveloped in clouds so dense that a strong sense of suffocation was absolutely produced. We all halted; the Canadians admitted that further progress was impossible; but the friendly shelter of the forest was at hand, and the pines waved their dark branches in token of an asylum. We turned our shoulders to the blast, and, comfortless and weather-beaten, sought our refuge. The scene, though changed, was still not without interest: the frequent crashes of falling trees, and the cracking of their vast limbs, as they rocked and writhed in the tempest, created awful and impressive sounds; but it was no time to be idle; warmth and shelter were objects connected with life itself, and the Canadians immediately commenced the vigorous application of their resources. By means of their small, light axes, a good-sized maple-tree was, in a very few minutes, levelled with the earth; and, in the mean time, we cleared

of snow a square spot of ground, with large pieces
of bark nipped from the fallen trees.   The fibrous
bark of the white cedar, previously rubbed to
powder between the hands, was ignited, and,
blowing upon this, a flame was produced.   This
being fed, first by the silky peelings of the birch
bark, and then by the bark itself, the oily and
pitchy matter burst forth into full action, and a
splendid fire raised its flames and smoke amidst a
pile of huge logs, to which one and all of us were
constantly and eagerly contributing.

"Having raised a covering of spruce boughs
above our heads, to serve as a partial defence from
the snow, which was still falling in great abundance, we sat down, turning our feet to the fire,
making the most of what was, under circumstances,
a source of real consolation. We enjoyed absolute
rest! One side of our square was bounded by a
huge tree, which lay stretched across it; against
this our fire was made; and on the opposite side,
towards which I had turned my back, another very
large one was growing, and into this latter, being
old and decayed, I had by degrees worked my
way, and it formed an admirable shelter. The
snow was banked up on all sides nearly five feet

high, like a white wall; and it resolutely maintained its position, not an atom yielding to the fierce crackling fire which blazed up close against it."

After preparing and feasting on an ample supper, the travellers lighted their pipes, and continued to smoke, till, dropping off by degrees, the whole party, except the chief, lay stretched out snoring. "Large flakes of snow continued to fall, and heavy clots dropped occasionally upon the ground. Our enormous fire had the effect of making me so comfortably warm, that I had deserted the use of my buffalo skin till I lay down to sleep; and were it not for the volumes of smoke with which I was at times disturbed, and the pieces of fire which burnt holes in my clothes wherever they happened to fall, my lodging would have been, under circumstances, truly agreeable. I sat for some time, with a blanket thrown over my shoulders, in silent contemplation of a scene alike remarkable to me for its novelty and its dreariness. The flames rose brilliantly, the sleeping figures of the men were covered with snow, the wind whistled wildly through the trees, whose majestic forms overshadowed us on every side, and our fire, while it shed the light of day on the immediately *surrounding objects*, diffused a deeper gloom over the farther recesses of the forest. And thus I remained without any inclination to sleep till it was near midnight. A solemn impression, not to be called melancholy, weighed heavily upon me. The satisfaction with which I regarded the fatigue which had gone by was hardly sufficient to inspire confidence as to what was to come; and this reflection it was, perhaps, that gave a colour to my thoughts at once serious and pleasing. Distant scenes were brought to my recollection, and I mused on past-gone times, till my eyes became involuntarily attracted by the filmy, wandering, leaves of fire, which, ascending lightly over the tops of the trees, for a moment rivalled in brightness the absent stars, and then—vanished for ever! .... I became overpowered with sleep, and, wrapping my buffalo skin around me, sank down to enjoy for several hours sound and uninterrupted repose. I slept heartily till day-light, when I awoke, feeling excessively cold, and found the whole party sitting up. The snow had ceased to fall, the sky had brightened, and intense frost had set in."

The dangers of the Alps have been often told, with especial relation to the noble dogs employed on the Great St. Bernard, to rescue travellers *from the perilous* passages in that vicinity. Snow-storms in Alpine districts are as sudden as they are terrific. After days of cloudless beauty, the sudden roar of the tempest, the fall of avalanches,

THE GREAT ST. BERNARD.

and the drifting of wintry snows, overtake the traveller with unexpected fury, and block up the road he is pursuing. Near the top of the Great

St. Bernard is the far-famed convent, whose hos-
pitable monks, and the fine race of dogs they keep
up in their establishment, have been so often
described by grateful travellers.   The keen scent,
and admirable docility of these dogs, are called
into action at a time when no human help could
otherwise reach the unhappy traveller.   Overwhelmed by a snow-drift, he lies perishing beneath a mass of perhaps ten or twenty feet in
depth, where.no sagacity of man could ascertain
his sad condition.   But these dogs with their
wonderful delicacy of smell can detect the fact,
and fix on the very spot where he lies buried.
Scratching up the snow with their feet, and utter-
ing at the same time a continued and deep bark,
they bring the courageous monks to aid in the
work, and either rescue the sufferer before life is
extinct, or dig up the body to be recognized by
friends.   But the dogs frequently penetrate spots
where it would be impossible for the monks to
follow them; and to provide for the chance of
their meeting in such situations with travellers in
distress, one of the dogs has a flask of spirits
round his neck, and another has a cloak to cover
the chilled limbs of the sufferer.   One of the dogs

of St. Bernard was long decorated with a medal, in commemoration of his having saved the lives of twenty-two persons. This noble creature died in 1816, in attempting to convey a poor traveller to his family, who dwelt at the foot of the mountain. It was during a very stormy season, and in descending the mountain, they were in an instant overwhelmed by two avalanches, which also destroyed the wife and children of the traveller who had set out to endeavour to obtain some tidings of him.

The most recent account of this interesting spot, and of the dangers to which it is exposed, is given in Murray's excellent Hand-book for Travellers in Switzerland, from which we give the following abridged extract:—

The Hospice is a massive stone building, well adapted to its perilous situation, which is on the very highest point of the pass, where it is exposed to tremendous storms from the north-east and south-west. This chief building is capable of accommodating seventy or eighty travellers with beds; three hundred may be sheltered; and between five and six hundred have received assistance in one day. Besides this, there is a house near the Hospice on the other side of the way;

it was built as a place of refuge in case of fire—
an event which has twice happened since the
foundation of the establishment. It is called the
Hôtel de St. Louis, in compliment to the Kings
of France, whose protection was often extended
to the Hospice. It is chiefly used for offices, and
for the domestics of the establishment. The
Hospice itself consists of a ground floor, occupied
by stabling and store-rooms,—a first floor, on
which are the chapel, the offices, and a long corridor,—and a second floor, on which are another
corridor, the dormitories, the refectory, and apartments for visitors. The principal room appro-
priated to visitors, is large and convenient; it is
hung with many drawings and prints, presents
sent by travellers in acknowledgment of the kind
attention which they had received from the brethren. A piano was among the presents thus sent
by a lady. Attached to this room is a cabinet, in
which a day, unfavourable to out-door pursuits,
may be passed with interest and pleasure. It contains collections of the plants, insects, and minerals
of the Alps, and many relics of a temple dedicated
to Jupiter, which formerly stood on this pass, near
to the site of the Hospice. The chapel of the

Hospice is generally well attended in fine weather by the peasants from the neighbouring valleys, and Alp pastures.   In this chapel there is a box, where donations in aid of the funds of the establishment are put; and travellers who receive its hospitalities, offer their acknowledgments in a sum not less than they would have paid for their accommodation at an inn.   The money thus given by those who can afford it ought to be in a more liberal degree, because that excess aids the monks to extend their assistance to poor and destitute travellers, a very numerous class of claimants upon them, from the great intercourse which exists by this pass between Switzerland and Italy.

There are usually ten or twelve brethren at the hospice.   They are young men who enter upon this service at eighteen, and devote themselves to it by vow, for fifteen years.   But they seldom survive the time of their vow ; the severities of the winters impair their health, and they are driven to retire to a lower and milder clime, but often with broken constitutions and ruined health.   Even in summer it has happened that the ice never melted in the lake on the summit, and in some years not a week has passed without snow falling. It always

freezes early in the morning, even in the height of
summer, and the Hospice is rarely four months
clear of deep snow. Around the building it
averages seven or eight feet, and the drifts sometimes rest against it and accumulate to the height
of forty feet. The severest cold recorded, was
29° below zero, of Fahrenheit; it has often been
observed at 18° and 20° below. The greatest heat
has been 68° in the height of summer. During
the severe cold the snow falls like dust; the particles are frozen so hard that they do not attach,
and form flakes as in the lower regions, nor harden
on the surface; a storm of wind, therefore, lifts
up the snow, and fills the air with it, like a mist
which the eye cannot penetrate. These are the
tourmentes so much dreaded by the poor wretches
exposed to their fury. Pedlars and smugglers
are almost the only travellers at the dangerous
season, when these are prevalent, and often are
they overwhelmed either by the tourmente or
the avalanche. At such seasons, undismayed by
the storm, the brethren of the Hospice seek amidst
these dangers the exhausted and overwhelmed traveller; they are generally accompanied by their
sagacious dogs. These do not roam alone, but are

useful companions to the brethren and their assist-
ants, by whose directions they traverse snow-heaps

THE *TOURMENTE*

and carry cordials to spots where the snow is too
slight to bear the weight of a man.

The dress of the brethren is a black cloth robe, which reaches nearly to the ankle, buttoned from top to bottom. A white slit band passes round the neck, the ends before and behind being tucked into the girdle. The head dress is a black conical cap with a tuft at the top. The white band on the neck is the distinguishing mark of the order of St. Augustine. The brethren are well-informed, kind, and courteous. They have a small library, and are also supplied with some periodical works. The language used by them is French, though there are Italians and Germans among them. During their short summers their intercourse with well-informed travellers is extensive, and thus they know what is passing in the world, from which they are self-excluded.

Supplies of provisions are brought to the Hospice from Aosta, and the neighbouring villages. The winter store of hay for the cows is so valuable that travellers are required either to bring their own provender for their mules, or to supply themselves from a salesman established in the convent. Wood for firing is brought from a forest four leagues distant, and its consumption is great; for at the elevation of the Hospice, water boils at about 190°, which is so much less favourable for cooking processes, that it requires five hours to effect that, which in lower regions, might be done in three.

The duties of the brotherhood of St. Bernard and their servants sometimes lead them into fatal danger. In the winter of 1825, a party of three maroniers, domestics of the convent, one of whom was Victor, a worthy man, well remembered by Alpine travellers, went out with two dogs to search, at a dangerous time, for travellers; they met one with whom they were returning to the convent, when an avalanche overwhelmed them, and all perished except one of the dogs, whose prodigious strength and activity enabled it to escape. The bodies of poor Victor and his companions were found after the melting of the snows in the following summer.

Avalanches are huge masses of snow or ice, which gradually become loosened from the mountain side, and are precipitated into the vallies beneath with tremendous force, sweeping away houses, trees, and every obstacle to their progress. The sides of the Jung-frau, the highest of the Bernese Alps, are described as being channelled

with furrows or grooves down which the avalanches descend with resistless force. As seen
from a distance, it is difficult to believe that the
fall of an avalanche can be so tremendous. A distant roar, as of thunder, announces its descent,
and in half a minute a gush of white powder re-
sembling a small cataract, is perceived issuing out
of one of the upper grooves or gullies; it then
sinks into a fissure and is lost for a time, but re-
appears some hundred feet below with another
roar, and a fresh gush from a lower gully, till the
mass of ice, reaching the lowest step, is precipitated into the gulf below. By watching attentively the sloping white side of the Jung-frau, the
mass of glacier, which produces this effect, may
be seen at the moment when disengaged, and
before the sound reaches the ear; sometimes it
merely slides down over the surface, at other times
it turns over in a cake; but in an instant after, it
disappears, is shattered to atoms, and in passing
through the different gullies, is ground to powder
so fine, that as it issues from the lowest, it looks
like a handful of meal, or a small cloud of dust.
The roar of an avalanche is an awful interruption
of the silence usually prevailing on the high Alps;

but it is difficult to believe that these echoing
thunders arise from so apparently slight a cause,
or that the cloud of dust is really the result of
whole tons of ice and snow, hurled down the
mountain with great velocity, and capable of
sweeping away forests, did any occur in their
course, and of overwhelming houses and villages. During the early part of summer, three
of these discharges may be observed on the Jung-
frau within an hour; in cold weather they are
less numerous, and in autumn they scarcely occur
at all.

> "The virgin mountain, wearing like a queen
> A brilliant crown of everlasting snow,
> Sheds ruin from her sides ; and men below
> Wonder that aught of aspect so serene
> Can link with desolation."

The snow-storms of the Pyrenees are exceedingly violent, and the force of the wind in many
of the defiles is tremendous. There is a proverb
among the mountaineers, that there "the son
never waits for the father, nor the father for the
son;" meaning, that the strong instinct of self-
preservation absorbs every other feeling in those
moments of danger. The fury of the wind raises
the snow from the ground like the waves of the
sea, or drives it forward like foam upon the waters.

English readers, who hear of the difficulties and dangers of these mountain roads in winter, may wonder why persons travel on them at that season of the year; why they do not wait till the time when the summer tourist frequents them; but it must be remembered that these roads are the common, and indeed the only, highways of the country, and that people pass over them on matters of business and necessity, more than for pleasure. Of those who travel over these roads, by far the greater number meet with no serious difficulty; the accidents which occur are frequent, and often fatal; but still they are only accidents, and do not prevent those who have business to perform from undertaking the journey. Thus the great military road over the Monte Stelvio is the only means of communication which the Emperor of Austria has to connect his German and Italian states, without violating the territory of another Government.

This road is a very interesting one, not only from its being the highest carriage-road in the world, but on account of the skill with which it is constructed, and the sublime scenery through which it passes. It is described as a singular and astonishing example of human labour. For *a considerable* distance half its width is covered in by strong wooden galleries, with roofs and supports sufficiently massive to resist the pressure of descending avalanches, which are very common here in winter. At one part of the road, soon after leaving Prad, the magnificent mountain of the Ortler Spitz,—the third of the European

THE ORTLER SPITZ.
From the summit of the Stelvio Pass.

mountains in height, 14,400 feet above the sea-
level,—opens suddenly to the view of the traveller,
" with a vast and appalling effect, as it is seen from
its extreme summit to its base, robed in everlasting
snows, which descend on its sides in enormous
glaciers, and stream into the valley below the road.
Immense masses of rocks, in themselves mountains, throw out their black and scathed forms,
in striking contrast with the brightness of the
glaciers which they separate." The Tyrolese side
of the pass is much steeper than the Italian, and
the road is formed into a series of zig-zags, in
order to preserve a gradual descent. By this
means, the fall never exceeds ten inches in a hundred. A post-house, built among these turnings,
was destroyed, in 1826, by an avalanche. It was
built with the utmost solidity, in order to resist
the weight of the falling snow; but the event
proved how feeble is the arm of man to contend
with " the avalanche,—the thunderbolt of snow,"
—for the house was smashed to atoms, and the
post-master found dead with a rock upon his
breast, which ten men could not move The two
ostlers, who were in the stable at the time, were
saved. It is supposed, that if the building had

been constructed with a sloping roof, so as to assist the descent of the avalanche, instead of opposing its progress, it might have escaped. On the summit of the pass, at a height of 9272 feet above the level of the sea, and 780 above the line of perpetual snow, stands a solitary house of refuge, one story high, inhabited by an inspector of the road. It is the highest permanent habitation in Europe. Other houses are established in convenient situations along the road, at some of which the traveller may find rest and refreshment; at others, only shelter.

But roads like these are much less dangerous than the paths which the hunter or the shepherd has to traverse over the glacier, among the upper valleys, in search of game, or of some green spot where the sheep and goats may find food during summer. We hear from many a summer tourist of the wonders and dangers of the glacier, but the dangers to which the hardy mountaineers are constantly exposed remain untold. In crossing the vast fields of ice in the elevated mountain regions, wide cracks or crevices gape upon the traveller, and threaten destruction; or they are often hid by a treacherous bridge of snow, which

yields to the foot, and hurls him into an icy grave.
Mr. Auldjo, during his ascent to the summit of
Mont Blanc, approached a crevice covered with a

BRIDGE OF SNOW.

bridge of snow, into which the leading guide plunged
his baton; he then proceeded one step and plunged.

again for the second, but his pole slipped from his hands, and fell through the snow into the gulf beneath, and he had only time to spring back on the ice, when the whole bridge, which he was attempting to pass, fell in. The Grand Plateau,— as the largest of the plains of ice on the mountain is called,—is intersected by some large crevices. In one of these crevices, fifteen or twenty feet wide, was found a bridge of snow, which proved strong enough to bear several persons at once, and, from its position in the chasm, it afforded shelter from the wind, which is extremely piercing at this elevated situation. The crevice, as seen from the edge, appears of immense depth, and its great breadth affords an opportunity of examining it. Mr. Auldjo says, " The layers of ice forming the glacier, varying in colour from deep blueish-green to a silvery whiteness, with myriads of long clear icicles hanging from all the little breaks in the strata, presented a scene of the greatest beauty." From a certain point, a little below the bridge, he was enabled to get a view of it: " the manner in which it hung suspended, with all the guides sitting on it, many hundred feet from the bottom of this stupendous chasm, was a beautiful and curious,

but at the same time an appalling sight. In one
moment, without a chance of escape, the fall of
the bridge might have precipitated them into the
gulf beneath. Yet no such idea ever entered the
imagination of my thoughtless but brave guides,
who sat at their meal singing and laughing, either
unconscious or regardless of the danger of their
present situation."

CHAPTER II.

HAVING described some of the dangers of travelling
in snowy regions, and some of the disastrous effects
produced by the beautiful and apparently harmless substance called snow, it is now time to consider its real nature.

When a cold current of air meets with the
vapour contained in a warm current of air, it
causes that vapour to fall in the form of rain,
snow, or hail. The state of the atmosphere deter-
mines which of these forms it shall take. Snow is
formed by the freezing of watery particles in the
lower regions of the atmosphere, which are at first
mere icy lines or stars, but collect together, and
form flakes, in the course of their descent to the

D

earth.   The formation of snow is often carried on
before the eyes of the dwellers in arctic regions.
Though they stop every crevice in their huts in
order to keep out the cold air, yet the walls are
covered with icy particles ; and, when a stream of
air accidentally finds entrance, snowy flakes are
precipitated.   The same curious sight has been
witnessed at St. Petersburgh.   In a crowded as-
sembly-room in that capital, a gentleman happened
to break a pane of glass, and the stream of intensely cold air, which entered by that means, was
sufficient to congeal the vapour in the air of the
room, which immediately fell in the form of snow-
flakes.   The Dutch who wintered in Nova Zembla
found that snow-flakes were formed from the
vapour of their breath, every time they came in
contact with the external air.

The snow that falls in northern latitudes is more
like a thick sleet than the large flakes which we
see in England.   The particles being frozen as
they descend, assume the form of minute crystals,
which, in a strong wind, are carried along in a
similar manner to the sand over the African deserts.
This appearance in the north is called a *snee-fog,* or
snow-fog.   Among the Alps of Switzerland it is

called *La tourmente*, or " the torment" as already described. Sometimes, when the sun shines brightly after a heavy fall of snow, and the cold prevents moisture from appearing, small polished plates of ice may be seen on the surface of the snow, refracting the light in colours as brilliant and varied as those of dew. On the borders of frozen pools, and on small bodies which happen to be fixed in the ice, and project from its surface, may be found groups of feathery crystals of curious and delicate forms.

As soon as snow reaches the ground it begins to change; it gradually loses its light flaky character, and becomes more and more solid. The adhesive quality of snow, at particular times, arises from its crystalline texture, aided by moisture which freezes in the mass. Snow sometimes displays beautiful blue and pink shades at sunset, as is observed with so much admiration on the Alps of Switzerland. It also reflects so much light from its surface as to enable persons to travel at night with the greatest ease.

Flakes of snow, as seen in temperate climates, are generally irregular in their shape, though often elegant and reflecting with great splendour the

rays of the sun. This is also the case in the
arctic regions, when the temperature of the air is
near the freezing point, and much snow falls.
Sometimes it consists of small grains; sometimes
of large, rough, white flakes; at others the flakes
are composed of rude, starry crystals, formed
of separate grains. But in severe frosts, although
the sky may appear perfectly clear, flakes of snow,
of the most regular and beautiful forms, are always
seen floating in the air, and sparkling in the sun-
beams; and the snow which falls in general is of
the most elegant texture and appearance. Many
are the wonders discovered to us by the microscope, both in the animal and vegetable world; but
it is doubtful whether there is anything among
these wonders to surpass in beauty the snow-flakes
of the polar regions. Even without the help of
the microscope, and in less rigorous climates, much
of this beauty is to be seen. Dr. Grew, who made
his observations on snow, nearly two hundred years
ago, declares that he who will go abroad with his
eyes " well fixed, and with good caution, and this
in a thin, calm, and still snow, may by degrees
observe, that many parts hereof are of a regular
figure, for the most part as it were so many little

rowells or stars of six points, and upon each of
these six points are set other points." Star-like
figures appear to be also the most common in polar
regions; and of these there are several interesting
varieties, as will be seen by the accompanying
figures, of which it is necessary to explain, that
the smaller markings are not intended as shadings,
but actually occurred in the snow crystals, though
with this difference, that the lines which appear
black in the figures were all white in the originals.
It is to Mr. Scoresby's researches in arctic regions,
that we are chiefly indebted for a knowledge of
these wonders; and it must have been, indeed,
a delicate task to make drawings of the several
forms, and to preserve the particles from melting
under the influence of the breath. So early as
1740 some of the crystals represented had been
described and figured by Dr. Nettis of Middle-
burgh, who gathered in one day twenty varieties,
and in two or three days following eighty more.
These were hard and transparent, and were received on a pencil, and placed on a piece of plate
glass, under the object-glass of a fine microscope.
Great care was taken not to allow the smaller particles to dissolve, either from the breath or the

SNOW CRYSTALS.

SNOW CRYSTALS.

warmth of the hand. Wonderful, indeed, is the
beauty bestowed on these objects, so extremely
small, and so soon to vanish away. Mr. Scoresby
divides the various crystals into five classes: the
first are those which are *lamellar,* or arranged in
plates. They are found in those regions in all
states of the air, and in great abundance. Most of
the specimens are extremely thin and transparent,
and of an exquisitely delicate structure. Some of
them are starlike, with six points; some are regular hexagons, or six-sided figures, of simple transparent plates; others are beautifully variegated
by white lines, forming smaller hexagons, or other
regular figures; others, again, are an accumulation
of hexagons, of immense variety: some of these
have spines and projecting angles of great beauty.
The second class consists of crystals, in which,
from a little plate or sphere in the centre, proceed
a number of branches in all directions. The third
are six-sided prisms: these are sometimes very
delicate and crystalline; at others white and
rough. The finest specimens, which resemble
white hair cut into lengths, not exceeding a
quarter of an inch, are so small and clear, that the
exact figure is not readily determined. The fourth

are six-sided pyramids; and the fifth are prisms, having one or both extremities inserted in the centre of a plate-like crystal. These are very rare, and most resemble a pair of wheels united by an axletree. The figures here represented are magnified from thirty to about four hundred times. The greatest quantity of crystals were observed to fall when the thermometer stood between 16° and 22°, and the wind was N.E. or NN.E.

When Dr. Clarke was in St. Petersburg, he noticed a beautiful example of the snow-crystal. The thermometer stood at 23° Fahrenheit, and there was no wind. "Snow, in the most regular and beautiful crystals, fell gently on our clothes, and on the sledge, as we were driving in the streets. All of them possessed exactly the same figure and the same dimensions. Every particle consisted of a wheel or star, with six equal rays, bounded by circumferences of equal diameters: they had all of them the same number of rays, branching from a common centre. The size of each of these little stars was equal to the circle presented by dividing a pea into two equal parts. This appearance continued during three hours, in which time no other snow fell, and there was sufficient leisure to examine them with the strictest attention, and to make the representation given at *a* in the figure."

In North America, snow has occasionally been observed in the form of cylinders or spheres; but this was an after effect, produced by a second shower falling on one which had previously fallen, and had been coated over with ice. A rough wind, causing the new snow to roll over this icy covering, formed it into balls and cylinders of various

sizes. Some of the latter are stated to have been
two or three feet in diameter.

The lightness of snow is occasioned by the extent of its surface very much exceeding the matter
it contains. It has been calculated that a flake of
snow, taken as nine times more expanded than
water, descends three times as slow. A depth of
twenty-seven inches of snow, in melting, does not
give more than three inches of water. The whiteness of snow is owing to the minute particles into
which it is divided; hence, when ice is pounded,
it is equally white. But although, in this country,
we associate the idea of the purest whiteness with
snow, yet there are districts of several miles in
extent, in arctic regions, and also among alpine
heights, where the snow is not white, but of a
reddish colour. Captains Parry and Ross have
both testified to this fact, and many scientific men
have given their testimony to the occurrence of
red snow among the Alps. It has been also ascertained that the red colour arises from the presence
of a vast multitude of minute bodies, of which
some are vegetable, but by far the larger portion
are animal. The latter are endowed with swiftness of motion, and are exceedingly curious objects

as seen through the microscope. The surface of
the snow is tinged with this rosy hue to the depth
of two or three inches, and sometimes a foot.
Mountain-snow is sometimes seen of a brown
colour, but this arises from its being mixed with
earthy substances brought from the superior heights
during the thawing of ice and snow. It is recorded,
on authentic testimony, that snow has been found
to exhibit a luminous appearance. A party in
Argyleshire, who were taking a pleasure excursion
on Loch Awe, were overtaken by a snow-shower
in March, 1813, and, to their astonishment, found
that the flakes were luminous, that they remained
so after they had settled on the sides of the boat
and on the dresses of the persons present. When
they touched this snow, their hands remained
luminous for some time after, although there was
no perceptible heat. It has been conjectured that
this effect was due to electricity, but it has not
been satisfactorily explained.

In countries lying within ten degrees of latitude
from the poles, the ground is always covered with
snow, even when its level is only a few inches
above the sea. And, in every part of the world,
there is a certain height at which the atmosphere

is in a state to form snow, and where, if land occurs, it will be covered with snow all the year round. This is called the *snow-line,* or limit of perpetual snow. Thus, we find that, in temperate and warm countries, the summits of lofty mountains, reaching to this height, are always covered with snow. The snow-line varies exceedingly: near the equator, it is three miles above the sea-level; in places that are equally distant from the equator and the poles, one mile and three quarters; and, near the poles, the snow-line comes down to the surface of the earth.

In our own country, the greatest falls of snow are in the months of December, January, and February; but, in general, these do not remain long on the ground. Close observers have noticed that snow sometimes disappears without any apparent thaw; or so much of it dissipates as to leave furrows in the general mass. This is attributed to evaporation, which will occur even below the freezing point. One hundred grains of light snow have been found to lose sixty grains in weight, during one night, when the temperature was below twenty-five degrees. This evaporation from snow is supposed to supply the water for the formation of those thin mists which appear during intense frost.

The uses of snow to the earth are many and most important.   Even on the summits of lofty mountains, where no sign of vegetation appears, but where snow always covers the heights, a most beneficial effect is produced on the surrounding countries, especially in such as are subject to peri- odical droughts of many months duration.   The partial melting of the mountain-snows, during summer, gives rise to numerous rivers, and keeps up the supply of their waters, to the vast benefit of the inhabitants of the regions through which they flow ; dispensing gladness and fertility around, and enabling the more industrious and civilized cultivators to irrigate their fields, and multiply the produce of their land.   At lesser elevations, snow has valuable uses to the vegetable world, in protecting it, during the winter season, from the effects of intense frost ; for, being a bad conductor of heat, it retains the temperature of the ground at what it was when the snow fell.   While the air above the snow may be 38° below zero, the ground below will only be at zero.   Hence the fine, healthy green colour of young wheat and young grass after the snow has melted in spring. In districts where snow remains on the ground all the winter, and only disappears with the approach of spring, this effect is much more obvious than with us; numerous beautiful and somewhat delicate plants, as auriculas, saxifrages, &c. flourish as wild flowers among the Alps, while with us the winter season is often destructive to them. This is easily accounted for, when we consider that, in their native heights, severe as they are, these plants have a covering, like that of a thick woollen garment, protecting them from frost during the whole winter; while, in this climate, they are exposed to sudden changes of temperature, being at one time drenched with long-continued rains, and at another, perhaps, exposed to severe frost, before any snow has fallen to shelter them. Occasional mild weather, during our winters, often causes plants to send out ill-timed shoots, and to commence a growth which is soon to be cut short again by nipping frosts. This weakens, if it does not destroy, the whole plant, and its summer flowering is greatly injured thereby.

ESQUIMAUX BUILDING SNOW-HUTS.

CHAPTER III.

WHILE the inhabitants of the south are quenching
their feverish thirst, and finding refreshment and
delight in the coolness imparted by snow, the
natives of polar regions apply the same substance
to the very opposite purpose of affording them
shelter and warmth. Captain Parry found the
huts of the Esquimaux to be made of no other
material than snow or ice, and some of them were
built with considerable skill. The methods adopted
by these ingenious builders, as witnessed by him,
are as follows:—" The work is commenced by

E

cutting from a drift of hard and compact snow a
number of oblong slabs, six or seven inches thick,
and about two feet in length, and laying them
edgeways on a level spot, also covered with snow,
in a circular form, and of a diameter from eight to
fifteen feet, proportioned to the number of occu-
pants the hut is to contain. Upon this, as a foundation, is laid a second tier, of the same kind, but
with the pieces inclining a little inwards, and made
to fit closely to the lower slabs, and to each other,
by running a knife adroitly along the under part
and sides. The top of this tier is now prepared
for the reception of a third, by squaring it off
smoothly with a knife; all which is dexterously
performed by one man, standing within the circle,
and receiving the blocks of snow from those employed in cutting them without. When the wall
has attained a height of four or five feet, it leans
so much inward as to appear as if about to tumble
every moment; but the workmen still fearlessly
lay their blocks of snow upon it, until it is too high
any longer to furnish the materials to the builder
in this manner. Of this he gives notice by cutting
a hole close to the ground in that part where the
door is intended to be, which is near the south

side, and through this the snow is now passed.
Thus they continue, until they have brought the
sides nearly to meet, in a perfect and well-con-
structed dome, sometimes nine or ten feet high in
the centre; and this they take considerable care
in finishing, by fitting the last block, or *key-stone*,

ENTRANCE TO SNOW-HUT.

very nicely in the centre, dropping it into its place
from the outside, though it is still done by the
man within. The people outside are, in the mean

time, occupied in throwing up snow with the snow-
shovel, and in stuffing in little wedges of snow
where holes have been accidentally left."

The builder next lets himself out by enlarging
the door-way to the height of about three feet.
Two passages are then built, each about ten or
twelve feet long, the floor of which is lower than
that of the hut. These passages sometimes connect two or three huts together, and are common
to the inhabitants of each. For the admission of
light, a round hole is cut on one side of the roof
of each apartment, and a circular plate of ice let
into it. The light is soft and pleasant, like that
transmitted through ground glass, and is quite
sufficient for every purpose. When, after some
time, these edifices become surrounded by drift, it
is only by the windows that they could be recog-
nised as human habitations. Their external appearance at night is very singular, when they are
discovered by a circular disk of light transmitted
through the windows from the lamps within.

Round the interior of each hut is raised a bank
of snow, which serves for the bed. The snow is
first covered with small stones, over which are
laid the paddles, tent-poles, and some blades of

whalebone; above these are placed a number of little pieces of net-work, made of thin slips of whalebone; and, lastly, a quantity of twigs of birch. Deer-skins can now be spread without risk of their touching the snow; and such a bed, says Capt. Parry, is capable of affording not merely comfort, but luxurious repose, in spite of the rigour of the climate.

The lamp is a shallow vessel of clay, and the wick is made of dry moss. A long thin slice of whale, seal, or sea-horse blubber, is hung up near the flame, the warmth of which causes the oil to drip into the vessel. This lamp gives a brilliant and beautiful light, without any perceptible smoke or offensive smell. Immediately over the lamp is a frame-work of wood, from which the cooking vessels are suspended; and it also serves to support a large hoop of bone, having a net stretched tightly within it, for the reception of any wet things, such as boots, shoes, and mittens.

When the lamps were lighted, and the hut full of people and dogs, Capt. Parry found the temperature of the air just over the net to be 38°; two or three feet from this it was 31°, or just below freezing point; close to the wall it was 23°,

while in the open air the temperature was 25°
below *zero.* A greater degree of warmth within
the huts produces extreme inconvenience, by the
dropping from the roofs. This is prevented by
applying a little piece of snow to the place from
which a drop proceeds; and this, by freezing, prevents further thawing, for a time at least. But
for several weeks in the spring, when the weather
is too warm for snow huts and too cold for tents,
the Esquimaux suffer much on this account.
Another remedy is to increase the height of the
huts, or add others, that they may be less crowded.
In building a higher hut, they construct it over,
and as it were concentric with the old one, which
is then removed from within. "It is curious,"
remarks Capt. Parry, "to consider that, in all
these alterations, the object kept in view was *coolness,* and this in houses formed of snow!" Describing a visit to these extraordinary abodes, he
says, "After creeping through two low passages,
having each its arched doorway, we came to a
small circular apartment, of which the roof was a
perfect arched dome. From this, three doorways,
also arched, led into as many inhabited apartments,
one on each side, and the other facing us as we

entered. The construction of this inhabited part
of the huts was similar to that of the outer apartment, being a dome formed by separate blocks of
snow, laid with great regularity and no small art,
each being cut into the shape requisite to form a
substantial arch, from seven to eight feet high in
the centre, and having no support whatever but
what this principle of building supplied. A cheer-
ful and sufficient light was admitted by a circular
window of ice, neatly fitted into the roof of each
apartment." Such was the appearance of these
huts soon after they were built, but in a month's
time they had altered for the worse. "The roofs
were much blackened by the smoke of the lamps,
and the warmth had in most parts given them a
glazed and honey-combed surface; indeed, the
whole of the walls had become much thinner by
thawing, so that the light was more plainly visible
through them. The snow, also, on which the lamps
stood, was considerably worn away, so as to destroy
in a great measure the regularity of the original
plan of construction." A little later, and it is
added, "Almost the whole of these people were now
affected with violent colds and coughs, occasioned
by a considerable thawing that had lately taken

place in their huts, so as to wet their clothes and
bedding; though as yet we had experienced no
great increase of temperature. From the nature
of their habitations, however, their comfort was
greater, and their chance of health better, when
the cold was more severe."

The Esquimaux hunter is so skilful in con-
structing snow walls, that he frequently erects one
to protect himself from the weather while watching the seal. This wary animal passes much of
its time in the water, in the pursuit of its prey,
and it has the power of inhaling a sufficient quantity of air to serve for a long period; when it
requires a fresh supply of air, it bores a passage
through the ice, and produces a rising in the snow
like a common mole-hill. When the Esquimaux
is hunting for seals, he frequently places his head
down on the ice to listen for the animal. If it
appears to be working up to the surface, the man
remains on the spot, and seldom quits it without
capturing the seal. " For this purpose he builds
a snow-wall about four feet in height to shelter
him from the wind, and seating himself under the
lee of it, deposits his spear, lines, and other imple-
ments, upon several little forked sticks inserted in

the snow, in order to prevent the smallest noise being made in moving them when wanted. But the most curious precaution to the same effect, consists in tying his own knees together, with a

ESQUIMAUX WATCHING A SEAL HOLE.

thong, so securely as to prevent any rustling of his clothes, which might otherwise alarm the animal. In this situation a man will sit quietly, sometimes for hours together, attentively listening to any noise made by the seal." The hunter ascertains that the seal has not taken alarm and abandoned the place, by means of a slender rod of bone, nicely rounded, having a point at one end and a knob at the other. This is thrust into the ice, and the motion of the part above the ice informs the hunter that the animal is still at work: if the knob remains undisturbed, the attempt is given up in that place; but it usually happens that the animal is not aware of the noiseless presence of its enemy. When the hunter supposes the hole to be nearly completed, he cautiously lifts his spear, and as soon as the blowing of the seal is distinctly heard, and the ice consequently very thin, he drives it into the animal with the force of both arms, and then enlarges the opening in the ice to enable him to get at his prey.

If snow is serviceable as a building material, it also forms the best and most compact roads for winter travelling, while in a case of necessity, a hummock of ice may supply the material of the travelling carriage itself. An Esquimaux woman who had volunteered her services to Captain Parry's party, in a visit to Winter island, found the distance too great for her son to walk. She

therefore set one of her friends to work among the
hummocks of ice upon the beach, from which a
neat and serviceable little sledge was soon cut out,
hollowed like a bowl or tray, and smoothly rounded
at the bottom. The thong to which the dogs were
attached, was secured to a groove cut round its
upper edge; and the young Esquimaux, seated in
this simple vehicle, was dragged along with great
convenience and comfort.

In North America numerous vehicles are used
for travelling on snow, under the general name of
sleighs. In the interior of the country, long journeys are seldom undertaken except during winter:
the roads being nearly impassable at any other
season, on account of their many imperfections
and the want of bridges. But when the frost has
completely set in, and snow has filled up the hollows, and ice has bound the streams, travelling
can be performed with ease and safety. This is
also the leisure season of the year, when farming
operations are suspended, and household cares are
diminished. When the snow is two or three feet
deep, wheel carriages are quite useless, and it is
then that the sleigh is in universal request. In
some districts, where snow seldom falls in suffi-

cient quantities to admit of sleighing, the inhabitants are overjoyed at a heavy snow-storm, and immediately arrange their several journeys. The horses in the sleighs have small bells hung on the harness; the sound of which is said to cheer the

THE SLEIGH.

animal as well as his master. In a frosty night, when sound is distinctly conveyed, the tinkle of the

leigh bells is heard at a great distance by an
ttentive and listening ear. The following lines
y Mrs. Moodie, prettily express the cheering
nfluence of that sound in a Canadian winter :—

SLEIGH BELLS.

'Tis merry to hear at evening time,
By the blazing hearth the sleigh-bells chime ;
To know each bound of the steed brings near,
The form of him to our bosoms dear.
Lightly we spring the fire to raise,
Till the rafters glow with the ruddy blaze.

'Tis he—and blithely the gay bells sound,
As his steed skims over the frozen ground.
Hark ! he has passed the gloomy wood,
He crosses now the ice-bound flood,
And sees the light from the open door,
To hail his toilsome journey o'er.

Our hut is small, and rude our cheer,
But love has spread the banquet here;
And childhood springs to be caress'd,
By our beloved and welcome guest ;
With smiling brow his tale he tells,
They laughing, ring the merry bells.

From the cedar swamp the wolf may howl,
From the blasted pine loud whoop the owl ;
The sudden crash of the falling tree,
Are sounds of terror no more to me ;
No longer I list with boding fear,
The sleigh-bells' merry peal to hear.

In some of the extensive plains of Canada, the
horse is not so well fitted as the dog for travelling
over the snow ; and the Canadian often pays as
much as fifty pounds sterling, for three small, but
well trained, dogs.   Their value is indeed felt,
when, in the midst of an extensive plain, he is
overtaken by a storm of wind which tears up the
surface of the snow, and bears it along in clouds
which obscure the sun, and prevent him from seeing
the foremost of his dogs.   Ignorant of the direction of his home, the path leading to it covered in
many parts with snow to the depth of ten or twelve
feet, he has nothing to do but to trust to the sagacity
of his dogs; he sits quietly in his sledge and calls
upon them to advance ; for a time they drag him
in all directions, but he at length knows by the
barking of the leader, that the track has been re-
gained, and then, sweeping like the wind over the
slender crust of snow into which larger dogs would
sink and perish with fatigue, he is carried to a place
of safety.

But sometimes it is safer for the traveller to
remain quiet until the storm is over.   He then
takes off the traces, and gives the dogs a little
food; changes his mocassins, and puts on dry

socks; then rolling himself in his blanket or buffalo skin, and with his gun by his side, he lies down *deep* in the snow, and finds it a safe, warm, and comfortable bed, even when the thermometer is many degrees below zero, and when to sleep on its surface, even if wrapped in leather, would be certainly fatal. The dogs come and stretch themselves upon their master; the whole party are soon asleep, and, "in such a resting place," says Mr. Sloane, "many besides myself have spent a solitary, yet comfortable night, in the neighbourhood of wolves, with many miles between us and any other human beings, and risen next morning in health and strength to proceed on our journey, and to offer thanks to a watchful Providence who had not only protected us during the night, but who had led us back in our dreams to our distant country and homes, and who had surrounded us, while thus sleeping on our snowy couch, with the forms of the friends and companions most deserving of our love."

In the remote regions of the "Far West," the American Indians find the depth of the snow a great advantage in hunting the buffalo. In that country the winters are long, and severely cold;

and the horses cannot be brought into the chase
with any good effect. The snow frequently lies
to the depth of three or four feet, being blown
away from the tops and sides of the hills, which
are left bare for the buffaloes to graze upon, and
drifted into the ravines and hollows. When these
huge animals are pursued by their enemies, they
endeavour to plunge through the snow-drifts, but
being soon wedged in and unable to move, they
fall an easy prey to the Indians, who run lightly
upon the surface of the drift by means of their

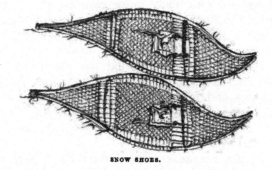

SNOW SHOES.

snow shoes, and pierce the animals with lances.
The skins are then stripped off, and sold to

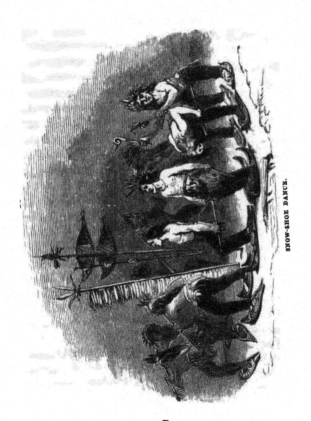

SNOW-SHOE DANCE.

F

the fur-traders, and the carcasses are left to be
devoured by the wolves. Great numbers of buffaloes are thus destroyed for the mere value of
their skins, which, in winter, are furnished with
abundance of long thick hair.   The snow-shoes of
the Indians differ in shape among the different
tribes, but are much the same as to materials.
They consist of a stout webbing made of stripes
of raw hide, and stretched over a frame-work of
elastic wood.   Thus they are so light as not to im-
pede the hunter, while they form such a resistance
to the snow as to carry the wearers along the surface without sinking in it.   At the beginning of
winter, and on the first fall of snow, the Indians
dance an exceedingly curious dance with the
snow-shoes under their feet, singing at the same
time, a thanksgiving to the Great Spirit, for send-
ing them a return of snow, when they can run on
their snow-shoes in their valued hunts, and easily
take the game for their food.*

Snow-shoes are commonly worn in Canada, in
snowy weather, whenever a journey has to be
taken.   A moderate-sized Canadian snow-shoe is

* Catlin.

a light wooden frame, of an oval shape, about forty inches long, and eighteen in extreme breadth, and its weight is about two pounds. The whole surface within is formed of a net-work of thong, like that of a racket, but rather stouter. A small square aperture, about the size of a man's hand, is left in the net-work, into which the toes sink at every step; by which means the foot is prevented from slipping back, and a purchase is given to step from, while the snow-shoe, forming an artificial platform, remains still on the ground. The foot is in no way confined to the machine, except by the toes, by which it is lifted, or rather dragged, along at each step. On these shoes the traveller passes over a surface of snow, perhaps twenty feet deep, in perfect safety. The snow-shoe makes a large track, and the leader of a party has the chief labour.

The use of snow-shoes is soon acquired, but a beginner is sure to suffer severely before he has learned the art of walking well in them. The complaint brought on by their use, in persons not trained to wear them from early youth, is called by the Canadians, *mal à raquette*, which is a violent inflammation and swelling of the instep and

ankles, attended with severe pain and lameness.
In frosty weather the snow-shoes are very heavy,
from getting clogged with ice.   It is necessary,
every now and then, to remove this by breaking it
off -with short sticks.   In places where there is
water under the snow, and the cold very severe,
the ice accumulates on the snow-shoes with great
rapidity: a large lump is apt to form under the
heel, causing the wearer to halt very frequently,
in order to get rid of it.   In such a case the foot,
at every step, seems as if chained to the ground.
The feet of the traveller are likewise protected by
mocassins.   Those of the common form are made
of ox-hide, and those of a better description of the
skin of the deer.   The hide of the moose-deer
furnishes the very best; but they are scarce, as
the animal, equal in size to the Russian elk, is of
a race nearly extinct: a few only are killed every
year in the spring, when there is a glassy surface,
or crust, over the snow hard enough to bear the
hunters on their snow-shoes, while it breaks in
under the heavy creature, which is thus easily
tracked by his foot-marks.   The mocassins intended for travelling are of a much larger size than
the common ones; for, besides other coverings, the

foot is wrapped in a piece of blanket, cut for the purpose, about fourteen inches long and eight wide, and then thrust into the mocassin, which is secured firmly by long thongs of soft leather passing round the ankles. As the upper part of the mocassin is composed of loose flaps, the foot has an excellent protection, and is kept warm and fit for the day's journey, either with or without snow-shoes.

Still more remarkable than the snow-shoes of the Indians, are the snow-skates of the Norwegians. During a considerable part of the year, Norway is covered with snow, and her winters extend to five or six months, and in the northern parts to a much longer period. At this time it is impossible to leave the beaten roads for the purpose at least of travelling; and when fresh snow happens to fall, even that means of communication is stopped, until the former track is opened for the sledge by means of the *snow-plough*, which will be described presently. The thinness, however, of the population, widely scattered over an immense extent of country, renders it, in many places, impossible to keep the roads open. It was natural, then, that the Norwegian should devise some mode by which

to leave his hut, generally far removed from roads,
and traverse forests, in various directions, with
sufficient swiftness to follow the chase, his favourite
occupation. For this purpose, he contrived the
skies, or snow-skates, which have been in use from
the earliest times. They consist of two thin nar-
row pieces of fir, of unequal lengths, the foremost
part being pointed, and turned upwards. The
longer, which measures about seven feet, is used

SNOW-SKATES AND SNOW-STAFF.

on the left foot; the other, which is about two feet
shorter, on the right. Each skate is about three
inches in width, and an inch in thickness in the

centre, where the foot is placed. To the sides of
the skate are fixed strong loops of willow, or of
fir-root, and through these are passed the leather
thongs which bind the skate to the foot. The
skates are smeared with tar or pitch; and on the
under side they are hollowed into a groove, to prevent slipping, and to enable the skater to keep a
straight course. They are also covered on the
under side with seal-skin, or pieces of rough boar's
hide, which gives an additional hold on the snow.
During the wars between Sweden and Norway,
the Norwegian light troops occasionally made use
of skates. Two regiments, in particular, were
trained to the use of these skates, and were called
Skielöbere, or skate-runners. This description of
soldiers is still in existence, though their numbers
are reduced. Bishop Heber thus describes them:
—" Two battalions of about six hundred men,
stationed in the north and south of Norway, are
drilled in the winter on skates; these men are
only called out twice a year, but they have frequent private drills for recruits. When they
exercise in skates, they have rifles slung, and
carry a staff in their hands, flattened at the end
to prevent it sinking into the snow, and to assist

them in the leaps they are sometimes compelled
to take when going down hill, (which, we were
told, they do with wonderful rapidity,) over such
obstacles as oppose their progress.   The only

SNOW-SKATERS.

difference in their method of drawing up is, that,
in winter, they allow between the files, room to
turn in the skates, which they do by changing
the right foot by an extraordinary motion which

would seem to dislocate the ankle." Another
writer, in describing these *Skielöbere,* says, " An
army would be completely in the power of even a
handful of these troops, which, stopped by no
obstacle, and swift as the wind, might attack it on
all points; while the depth of the snow, and the
nature of the country, would not only make any
pursuit impossible, but almost deprive them of
the means of defence, the *Skielöbere* still hovering
round them like swallows, skimming the icy surface, and dealing destruction upon their helpless
adversaries." When the snow is in good condition, the peasantry, as well as the soldiers, make
extensive use of these skates. On flat ground the
skater slides along at a tolerably good pace, much
faster than he could walk, as his feet do not sink
in the snow. His progress up hill is very slow
and fatiguing, and on hard snow he would slip backwards, but for the resistance of the hair on the under
part of the skates. But he descends the steepest
mountains in the most fearless manner, and with a
headlong speed which has been compared to that
of an avalanche: he has only to guide his flight
with a pole, so as not to run over a precipice. It
seems to require great dexterity and practice to

run well on these snow-skates.   On a common
road, a good skater will beat a horse in a sledge.
The skates are familiar to every Norwegian, without distinction of age or sex; and by means of
them the widely dispersed inhabitants repair, in
winter time, to church; traversing mountains,
lakes, and arms of the sea, as well as level ground,
and often saving three or four leagues of the distance they are obliged to travel at other seasons,
when ice and snow have not performed their work
of road-making.

The mountain guides of Switzerland are in the
habit of descending snow-hills by sliding down
them, as in the following cut.   Mr. Auldjo, on
his return from the summit of Mont Blanc, describes this rapid method of travelling.   He says:
" The first guide, finding the way clear and safe,
sat down on the edge of the declivity, and in an
instant slid on to the level below.   I was desired
to sit behind the second, as close as possible to
him, and to put my legs round his body, my feet
over his thighs, and my hands over his shoulders.
Thus placed, I kept fast hold of him, and away
both glided with immense velocity; he making
use of his baton as a kind of rudder to guide our

course, and with his feet ready to moderate the rapidity of our progress, by plunging them into the snow. This is a sort of Russian-mountain

SLIDING DOWN SNOW-HILLS.

sport, on a grand scale; and, on occasions like the present, is equally recommended for celerity and convenience. It often enabled us to shorten our route, by altering it for the opportunity of thus sliding down any declivity which we met with; passing in one moment over tracks which it had cost us an hour to climb. It excites merriment, from the tumbles and rollings-over which occasionally occur. Those who are sliding down less rapidly are often overtaken by those whose velocity is greater; and both are generally upset, and roll down together for some distance before they can get right again. When crevices are near the sides, or terminate the descent, it is dangerous, and no jokes are practised. The guide is very skilful in this manner of gliding down places nearly perpendicular. He can, in most cases, by the assistance of the baton, turn himself from any dangerous part, should he chance to meet with one, either running parallel with or intercepting his course, and can easily stop himself in time if it should be before him. This dexterity is extraordinary, considering the amazing velocity of the descent."

The guides have also another plan of descending snow-hills. Placing their feet together, they stand on the heel, and incline the body backwards, resting on the baton, which is placed under the left arm, and the point in the snow, at a proper distance behind, making a triangle, of which the body and the baton form two equal sides. Keeping this position during the whole descent, they slide down with wonderful celerity.

It has sometimes happened in England that a heavy fall of snow has blocked up the roads, and stopped the usual traffic. The inconvenience thus occasioned is very great; people cannot set about their ordinary work: goods and provisions cannot be sent from place to place, and people are delayed in their journeys and put to expense and inconvenience: but in our country this seldom lasts many days; men are sent to shovel off the snow from the roads, or a thaw causes it to melt. In the more northern countries, however, where the snow at the beginning of winter falls to a depth of several feet, and where the frost lasts many months, the opening of the roads after a fall of snow is a more difficult and important work. The machine generally used for this purpose is called a *snow-plough*, a sufficient idea of which will be given by the wood-cut, where it is shown set up against a tree. The plough being placed flat upon the ground, a horse drags the sharp end along, which by its wedge shape throws the snow on either side, and flattens and levels the remainder. This work is very hard, both for man and horse, especially when the fall of snow has been unusually

SNOW-PLOUGH.

heavy, and the country is hilly, as they have to wade through a depth of snow of some feet, for the purpose of dragging the plough along. Some attempts have been made in Sweden to improve this plough by lengthening the centre bar, and yoking oxen thereto, to push the plough before them, instead of dragging it after them: they would not thus be impeded by the depth of the snow. In Scotland, a snow-plough, similar in form to the above, is used for clearing tracks for the sheep along the hill sides. When the ground is covered with old snow, and the temperature of the air is above freezing, it is found that by stirring up the snow, it melts faster than it would if left to itself. A *snow-harrow* is therefore first used; this cuts the frozen snow into stripes of five or six inches broad, which are easily reduced to powder by the feet of the sheep, or divided by the snow-plough so as to open tracks for them.

Snow is not without its peculiar disadvantages and dangers to all who are long exposed to its influence. One of these is the painful and distressing malady called *snow-blindness.* This is occasioned by the glare of light reflected from the snow. The inhabitants of snowy countries have their own methods of guarding against this evil, and it is necessary for strangers to observe these, and carefully to use the same precautions. Captain Parry observed, that the Esquimaux were in

the habit of wearing wooden shades over the eyes,
and he therefore employed them in making these
articles for his own people, to be bartered for
other commodities which might be useful among
themselves.   But the crew did not always escape
the dreaded disease.   In an expedition in which
their eyes were much exercised in endeavouring
to distinguish the land from the ice, (both being
covered with snow,) the whole party became snow-
blind, so that no one was able to direct the sledge.
Their commander remarks, " I found a handkerchief tied close, but not too tightly round the
eyes, for a whole night, to be a much more effectual remedy for this disagreeable complaint than
any application of eye-water; and my companions
being induced to try the same experiment, de-
rived equal benefit from it." An aggravated form
of this disease seems to be prevalent in the snowy
regions of South America.   It is called by the
Peruvians *norumpi*, and is accompanied by dread-
ful pain. A pimple forms on the eye-ball, and
causes an itching pricking pain, as though needles
were continually piercing it. The sufferer becomes blind merely from not being able to open
the eyelids for a single moment, the smallest ray

of light being insupportable. The form of relief adopted in Peru is a poultice of snow, which must be frequently renewed, for, as soon as it melts away, the intolerable pain returns. When the division of Cordova marched from Cuzco to Pano, it halted at Santa Rosa, and, with the exception of twenty men and the guides, who knew how to guard against the danger of travelling in snowy districts, the whole division was struck blind: and this calamity occurred at the distance of three leagues from any human habitation. The guides galloped on to a village in advance, and brought a hundred Indians to assist in leading the men. Many of the sufferers, maddened with pain, had strayed away from the column, and perished before the return of the guides, who, together with the Indians, took charge of long files of the poor sightless soldiers, clinging to each other with desperate agonized grasp. During this dreary march by a rugged mountain path, several fell down the precipice and were never heard of more. The complaint, though exceedingly tormenting, seldom lasts more than two days.

Another inconvenience to which the traveller in snowy regions is exposed is that of *snow-*

G

thirst, or an earnest longing for water, and a
parched and burning state of the mouth and lips
similar to that of travellers in hot countries. In
attempting to satisfy his thirst by eating of the
snow that lies so plentifully around him, he only
increases his suffering, for snow, unless melted
over the fire and boiled, has not the refreshing
properties which are necessary to quench thirst.
In woods and sheltered places, it is easy for the
traveller to make a fire, and melt some of the
snow in a small pot or kettle, which he always
carries as a necessary part of his luggage; but in
the open plains no fire-wood is to be procured for
the purpose, and the frequent gusts of wind,
tearing up the surface of the snow, and driving
it along in dense clouds, would also prevent the
accomplishment of his object. Captain Parry
notices the remarkable thirst of the Esquimaux
race; and this is doubtless in some measure
owing to the cause just named. He says, "Their
only drink is water; and of this, when they can
procure it, they swallow an inconceivable quantity; so that one of the principal occupations of
the women during the winter, is the thawing of
snow in the ootkooseks for this purpose. They

cut it into thin slices, and are careful to have it
clean, on which account they will bring it from a
distance of fifty yards from the huts. They have
an extreme dislike to drinking water much above
the temperature of 32°."

In our own country, and in others of similar
temperature, it would appear strange to attach
much importance to the use of ice and snow in
cooling summer beverages; but, in the warmer
climates of the south, the case is far otherwise.
During the exhausting heat of summer, the poor-
est among the inhabitants of Naples would turn
away unrefreshed from a draught of water, or
even of wine, if he had not a handful of snow to
put into it; for it is snow, and not ice, that is
used for the purpose in the south of Italy. The
country itself is too warm, in the inhabited parts,
to supply that luxury; but its lofty mountains,
the chain of the Appenines, furnish an abundant
store of snow, which is diligently collected and
stored for use. For this purpose caves or pits are
dug in the sides of the mountains, especially on
the northern side; and into them is thrown, in
the proper season, a quantity of broad, thick layers
of snow. These are well pressed together until

the cave is full, when the opening is filled up with branches of trees, dried leaves, or straw, and sometimes a rude stone building is erected over it. A few of the loftiest summits of the Appenines rise above the snow-line, and are therefore covered with snow all the year round; but from the lower ridges the snow melts away in summer, and it is only by the exercise of industry and art that the inhabitants of the surrounding country are able to ensure the continuance of this luxury throughout the summer. The lower down the mountain the snow-cave is made, the less trouble in getting it at the season when it is most wanted, but the greater risk of its melting away. The situation must, therefore, be well chosen, and the spot well shaded by trees, or by some projecting portion of rock, which may keep off the rays of the sun. It happens, on rare occasions, that a snow-shower of considerable thickness will fall, during winter, on the lower and inhabited ridges. When this occurs, it is a cause of general rejoicing; for it saves the labour of collecting it from the heights. Men, women, and children, rush out with shovels, baskets, &c., to collect the falling treasure. They sing, shout, and laugh, gathering in their harvest

of snow at the same time. Immense snow-balls
are made, but not to be thrown about in pastime ;
they are carefully rolled, by children, to the caves
in the mountain-side. If the snow-harvest gives
employment to numbers of the peasantry in
winter, the conveyance and sale of the same substance, in summer, is also a source of constant
activity. The task of bringing snow from the
mountain-caves, and distributing it in the various
shops of Naples which are opened for the sale of
that article alone, is one which is carried on during
the night. Mules are loaded with the fragile
burden at the caves' mouths, and convey it down
the mountain to the boats, which take it into
Naples, where it is deposited in a large, cool
building, called " *La Dogana della neve,*" or the
snow custom-house, where retail dealers come
from all parts of the town to supply themselves. The snow-trade is in the hands of government, and produces a considerable revenue. The
dealers are bound to sell the snow at a fixed price,
and are fined if they do not bring a sufficient
supply. Few things, it is said, would be more
likely to produce a revolt among the peasantry
than a deficiency of snow in the dog-days. The

snow-shops, of which there is one in nearly every
street in Naples, are kept open day and night
during the season; snow being used medicinally,
as well as for mere refreshment. Similar habits,
with respect to the collection and use of snow, are
prevalent in Sicily, where the great storehouse of
snow is Mount Etna.

CHAPTER IV.

THE animals of snowy countries are protected from the severity of the weather by an increase in the quantity, and a change in the colour of their fur. The greater their exposure to the cold, the thicker is the natural covering bestowed upon them. This is so well known to dealers in fur, that they will only buy the skins of those animals which are known to have been killed in winter. Indeed the fur of North American animals killed in summer is unfit for purposes of commerce, being decidedly of inferior quality. This is also the case with skins procured in the early part of winter, or during a season of unusual mildness. There is another reason why some of the most costly furs must always be procured in mid-winter: it is only during that season that they attain the peculiar colour for which they are valued. The ermine, for instance, whose furry covering is every where highly celebrated and

PTARMIGANS.
(Summer and Winter plumage.)

regarded as the emblem of purity, is in summer
of a dingy yellow colour, and only puts on its
robe of snowy whiteness on the arrival of very
severe weather. There are other instances of this
remarkable change of colour in animals, such as
the Alpine hare and the Arctic fox. These change
from dusky grey, or ash colour, to white, the
rapidity of the change depending upon the severity of the season. One advantage to the
animals in this change is, that being like the
snow itself in whiteness, they are scarcely to be
distinguished from it, and have therefore some
chance of escape from their enemies. But the
great advantage lies in the fact, that a white surface does not permit the escape of heat so readily
as a darker one, and therefore the white animal
suffers less from cold in winter. Arctic animals
are thus enabled to bear a climate which would
otherwise, in all probability, be fatal to them;
and it is likewise inferred, from the researches
made in this curious subject by scientific men,
that at the same time that the hair of animals
undergoes this change,—namely, when the cold is
intense, and the days are dark,—the eyes also
become adapted to the faint light of arctic regions,

by losing the black pigment upon which the retina
is spread. Thus beautifully are the senses and
faculties of animals adapted by an all-wise Providence to the situations in which they are placed.
A greater degree of care seems to have been ex-
pended on the inferior animals in this respect, than
on man, whose body is by no means fitted to
endure all those variations of climate which
quadrupeds and birds can suffer without injury.
But on man have been abundantly bestowed those
higher gifts which enable him to provide for his
own safety, and to use such clothing, and take
such precautions as shall secure his body from the
effects of climate. We have seen how cleverly
the poor Esquimaux contrive their dwellings,
shutting themselves up in snow huts, which afford
the very best protection from the cold. Wrapped
in the thickest furs, and cheered by the light
of lamps fed with seal oil, these people enjoy
a degree of warmth and comfort scarcely to be
expected in their rigorous climate. Still more
cleverly does the inhabitant of civilized countries adapt his dress, his houses, his equipages,
and all which belongs to him, to the particular
climate in which he is placed; and if unexpected

circumstances arise, his reason soon teaches him how to act under them. When Captain Ross's crew were in danger of perishing amid the snows, after the shipwreck of their vessel, they set themselves to digging deep trenches in the snow. Across the top of these trenches they stretched and fixed some canvass, and upon the canvass they laid roofs of snow. Three trenches were thus made before night came on, each being large enough to contain seven persons. One officer and six men crept into each trench, having first constructed bags of double blanketing, into which they might get, and thus prevent their feet escaping into the snow while they slept. The bags were tied round their necks, and thus lying close together, they contrived to preserve life and warmth under a degree of cold varying from 62° to 92° below the freezing point.

The instances of protection from cold arising from a change of colour in animals, are not confined to quadrupeds. We may give one or two among birds, which are equally remarkable. The ptarmigan, an inhabitant of mountainous and snowy regions, has a beautifully mottled summer plumage of brown, grey, and white, with black

shafts to the wing and tail feathers. The winter
appearance of the same bird is thus described by
one of our ornithologists :—" As autumn advances,
the plumage begins gradually to change, the black
and brown giving way first, and then the grey,
till, by the time that the winter is confirmed, the
whole bird, with the exception of the eye streak
in the male, the outer tail feathers, and the shafts
of the middle ones, and the quills, becomes snow-
white. Those changes do not take place in con-
sequence of a moult, or separation of the coloured
feathers to be replaced by white ones, but by an
actual change of colour in the feathers themselves.
No doubt new feathers grow towards autumn, and
some of the old ones are thrown off; but there is
no general moult in the feathers at that season,
and probably not at any season, the moult being
gradual, just as the shedding of leaves is upon
some evergreen trees." * * * " That the autumnal
change of colour in the ptarmigan, and probably
also the summer change, is a change in the same
feathers, and not the effect of a moult, is proved
by many circumstances. In the first place, the
birds have a more powerful flight during the time
that the change is taking place than at any other

period of the year. In the second place, two
moults at least would be necessary; for, with the
exception of the ear-coverts, the prevailing tint of
the whole bird is grey in autumn, and brown in
summer. Thirdly, the decay, first of the brown,
and then of the grey, is gradual over the whole
bird. Fourthly, the change to white is complete
in proportion as the place and the season are cold.
The plumage of the ptarmigan is thus a sort of
natural thermometer; and as the plumage becomes
a bad conductor of heat in proportion as it
whitens, and the evaporating power of the air
diminishes with the cold, it is probable that the
birds may feel as warm while burrowing in the
snow as while basking in the sun."

The snow-bunting, otherwise called the snow-
bird, or snow-flake, is another instance of the
natural protection afforded by change of colour in
the plumage. It is a polar bird, and is therefore
subject to greater extremes of cold than even
the ptarmigan, which is a dweller on mountain
tops. Yet it wanders to more temperate climes
when the storms of polar regions have set in, and
have closed up its native pastures. When these
storms come early and suddenly on its accustomed

haunts, the bird is sometimes caught by them in its summer plumage, or with only the commencement of a change. In that state it is less prepared

THE SNOW-BUNTING.

to meet the cold, and hastily begins to migrate southward, when it is named, according to its appearance at that time, "tawny bunting," or "pied finch." But if the season be a more gradual

one, the bird remains long enough to acquire a
snowy appearance before it is compelled to go
southwards; and, under these circumstances, it ac-
quires a different name, and is often mistaken for
a different bird. The natural summer plumage is
of a tawny orange mixed with black; but in
winter the male bird is pure white, with the exception of some black markings on the back, and
on the wing and tail feathers. Sometimes these
birds arrive in the northern isles and highlands
of Scotland, appearing to be driven thither by the
violent north-east winds which precede a fall of
snow. On their first arrival they are very lean
and thin, and many of them perish in the wreaths
of snow; but when the storm abates, those which
reach the lower lands soon fatten and thrive. In
Lapland these birds are much prized as delicacies
for the table, and are caught in great numbers for
that purpose.

Snow-birds, and snow-animals, in general, have
thus a provision made for their safety, and are
enabled to withstand a degree of cold which would
be fatal to most of their race; but it is, perhaps,
equally surprising to the traveller in mountainous
regions to find that, at great elevations, on the

very verge of the glacier, and amidst fields of perpetual snow, beautiful and delicate flowers peep
forth under the influence of the brief but powerful
rays of a summer's sun. Some little spot from
which the snows have melted will often display
amidst the desolation and barrenness around, a
wondrous variety of flowers, and those of a kind
which are cherished as ornaments of flower-gardens
in milder situations. Gentians and lilies, hyacinths
and blue-bells, and the beautiful red rhododen-
dron, here flourish for a summer that only lasts a
few weeks. And beyond this lovely scene, where
at still greater heights the air becomes icy cold,
and all is snow, glacier, or rock, rising in a wild
and imposing solitude, where the cawing of a
raven, or the shrill cry of a marmot, is the only
sound that breaks the universal silence, even there
the hardy lichen may sometimes be seen covering
the rock. And so it is even in arctic regions;
flowers, indeed, are unknown, but lichens assume
a size and importance not witnessed in temperate
climates, and are also of great utility in affording
food to that useful animal the rein-deer. One
species in particular, commonly called rein-deer
moss, is the chief dependance of this animal, and

he is gifted with instinct to discover it, however deeply the ground may be covered with snow. Extensive plains, clothed with this lichen, are esteemed by the Laplander, in the same way that large and fair pastures are by us. And it has been so ordained by a wise Providence, that this humble plant should grow in such profusion as to afford an almost constant supply to these animals. The only occasion on which they suffer from the want of it is when the snow happens to have all melted away during the summer, and a sudden frost freezes up the lichen. The rein-deer then suffers extreme hardships, for he has no other resource, and he never touches hay. But this occurrence is very rare; the winter is almost always ushered in by heavy falls of snow, and these protect the plant from the rigours of the climate, while they do not bury it beyond the reach of the sagacious rein-deer, who knows both where to seek for it and how to scrape away the snow until he reaches it.

In our own country, few flowers venture, as in Alpine heights, to come forth from the very bosom of the snow; for the sudden changes of our climate and the severe frosts, which often occur when

H

the ground is unprotected by snow, are even more
trying to plants than the settled severity of Alpine
winters.   The snow-drop, however, is of that

THE SNOW-DROP.

hardy nature that it often appears in February
when the snow is still lying on the ground.   The
French give this flower the name of *Perce-neige,*

because it often pierces the snow.   The following
lines well express its hardy nature :—

> " Already now the snow-drop dares appear,
> The first pale blossom of the unripened year;
> As Flora's breath, by some transforming power,
> Had changed an icicle into a flower,
> Its name and hue the scentless plant retains,
> And winter lingers in its icy veins."

We are, perhaps, accustomed to consider the
inhabitants of snowy regions as an unfortunate
race, subjected to severe deprivations and positive
evils. But so wisely ordained are all the conditions
and circumstances of life, that the despised Esquimaux, or the diminutive Laplander, can command
a degree of comfort and enjoyment which might
seem impossible in their circumstances. In Captain Parry's account of the ingenious dwellings of
the Esquimaux, and the general amiability, frequent intelligence, and laborious industry of the
people, we have an instance which may teach us
not to consider any race of men, however apparently low or hard their lot, as either deficient in
the feelings and sympathies of mankind, or as in
any wise overlooked or hardly dealt with by their
Maker. The same wise, overruling Providence
watches over all; and the chief thing to be desired

in behalf of the untutored inhabitants of these wild and remote regions is, not that they should be taken from their present situation, and placed in what we should consider more favourable circumstances, but that the light of the Gospel may penetrate their dark abodes, and the worship of the Most High be established from pole to pole.

LONDON :—R. CLAY, PRINTER, BREAD STREET HILL.

CPSIA information can be obtained
at www.ICGtesting.com
Printed in the USA
BVOW06s2036300117
474854BV00020B/460/P